The Missions of California

Mission San Antonio de Padua

Kim Serafin

The Rosen Publishing Group's

TM

New York

Published in 2000 by The Rosen Publishing Group, Inc.
29 East 21st Street, New York, NY 10010

Photo Credits and Photo Illustrations: pp. title pg, 4, 14, 16, 18, 20, 25, 35, 44, 47–50 by Christina Taccone; pp. 5, 23, 24 © North Wind Archives; p. 6 © Museo Navale, Genua-Pegli/A.D.G., Berlin/Superstock; pp. 8, 19 © CORBIS/Bettman; p. 9 © Art Resource; p. 11 © Superstock; p. 12, 15 by Tim Hall; pp. 17, 41 © Department of Special Collections, University of Southern California Libaries; p. 27 © CORBIS/David Muench; p. 28 © Christie's Images/Superstock; p. 28 © CORBIS/Richard Cummins; pp. 30, 43 © Santa Barbara Mission Archive-Library; p. 31 (all) by Eda Rogers; pp. 32, 34, 45, 46; p. 36 by Gil Cohen; p. 39 © The Granger Collection; pp. 52, 57 by Christine Innamorato.

First Edition

Book Design: Danielle Primiceri

Layout: Kim Sonsky

Editorial Consultant Coordinator: Karen Fontanetta, M.A., Curator, Mission San Miguel Arcángel
Editorial Consultant: Dr. Robert L. Hoover, Ph.D.
          Professor Emeritus, Cal Poly, San Luis Obispo
          California Historical Resources Commission
Historical Photo Consultants: Thomas L. Davis, M.Div., M.A.
          Michael K. Ward, M.A.

Serafin, Kim.
      Mission San Antonio de Padua / by Kim Serafin.
          p.   cm. — (The missions of California)
      Includes index.
      Summary: Discusses the Mission San Antonio de Padua from its founding in 1771 to the present day, including the reasons for Spanish colonization in California and the effects of colonization on the local Indians.
      ISBN 0-8239-5489-7 (lib. bdg.)
      1. San Antonio de Padua (Mission)—History Juvenile literature. 2. Spanish mission buildings—California—King City Region—History Juvenile literature. 3. Franciscans—California—King City Region—History Juvenile literature. 4. Indians of North America—Missions—California—King City Region—History Juvenile literature. 5. California—History—To 1846 Juvenile literature. [1. San Antonio de Padua (Mission)—History. 2. Missions—California. 3. Indians of North America—Missions—California. 4. California—History—To 1846.] I. Title. II. Series.
      F869.S175S47   2000
      979.4'76—dc21
                                                              99-27378
                                                              CIP

Contents

Mission San Antonio de Padua

All along the coast of California, on a stretch of highway known as El Camino Real, sit the 21 Spanish missions. The key to much of California's rich history can be found in these settlements. Even though it was the third mission to be founded, San Antonio de Padua was the site of some California "firsts." The first marriage ceremony to be held in California was performed at Mission San Antonio de Padua. On May 16, 1773, Juan Maria Ruiz, age 25, was married to Margarita de Cortona, age 22. San Antonio de Padua was also the first California mission to make and use tiles on its buildings. The inhabitants of San Antonio de Padua built the first water-powered gristmill in California. The gristmill was a building where wheat was ground into flour. Water from the San Antonio River was directed to the mission and used to run the gristmill. As you can imagine, this was an important advancement for all of California's people. Mission San Antonio also had the first tile roof, the first extensive water system, and the first and only election in which the Indians were allowed to vote. From its beginning days, Mission San Antonio de Padua had a unique and interesting story.

A gristmill built by Indians at Mission San Antonio de Padua.

◀ *Mission San Antonio de Padua was the first to have tiled roofs.*

5

Before Europeans arrived in the area we now consider California, the land was already populated by many different groups of American Indians. In the area where San Antonio de Padua was built, there were 2,000 to 3,000 Indians who belonged to a tribe called the Salinan. When Christopher Columbus accidentally discovered the Americas, he put Spain in a good position to claim the land there. The king of Spain was first interested in this land because he believed that explorers might find a river that cut across the entire continent. He

Christopher Columbus

wanted to find a shorter route to Asia so that Spain could bring back riches like tea, silk, and spices.

In 1594, a Portuguese explorer named Sebastián Rodríguez Cermeño was sent by the Spanish government to look for ports on the California coastline. Cermeño was put in command of a large boat, called the *San Augustín*, but stormy weather along the coast caused damage to the boat. Cermeño was forced to return to Spain with the bad news that the boat and its cargo were destroyed.

In 1596, a Spanish sailor and businessman named Sebastián Vizcaíno made a bargain with the Spanish government. If it would allow him to look for pearls along the Pacific coast of America, he would look for good harbors on the land. Again, the explorers found trouble. Storms attacked the ship, the American Indians were

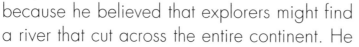

unfriendly, and food ran out. Vizcaíno, however, told the Spanish government that there were rich lands in California and that the Indians were happy to cooperate.

During the 1600s, Spain tried many times to begin colonization in California. In 1679, the Spanish government decided to pay the sailor Atondo y Antillón to make sure the job would be done. At first, a group of Catholic priests called Jesuits did the work of turning the Indians into Christians and Spanish citizens. The Jesuits created missions in New Spain, the land now called Mexico. Spain thought the Jesuits were becoming too powerful, and they found this threatening.

○ San Francisco de Solano
○ San Rafael Arcángel
○ San Francisco de Asís
  ○ San José

    ○ Santa Clara de Asís
○ Santa Cruz
  ○ San Juan Bautista
○ San Carlos Borromeo del Río Carmelo
○ Nuestra Señora de la Soledad

○ San Antonio de Padua
  ○ San Miguel Arcángel

○ San Luis Obispo de Tolosa

○ La Purísima Concepción
  ○ Santa Inés
    ○ Santa Bárbara
      ○ San Buenaventura

        ○ San Fernando Rey de España
          ○ San Gabriel Arcángel

            ○ San Juan Capistrano

              ○ San Luis Rey de Francia

                ○ San Diego de Alcalá

The Jesuit missionaries baptized Indians into the Catholic faith.

On June 24, 1767, the king of Spain ordered the Jesuits to leave New Spain. Franciscan friars took the Jesuits' place at the missions. The Franciscans were an order of Catholics who devoted their lives to doing charity and spreading the word of Catholicism. As a result, a new page in mission history began.

Mission San Antonio de Padua is named for Saint Anthony of Padua, who was born in Lisbon, Spain, in 1195. He was a generous man and a great preacher. During his lifetime he performed many miracles, which earned him the name "Wonder-Worker." Saint Anthony died in 1231 and was buried in Padua, Italy. He was canonized (made a saint) the next year and is considered the patron saint of the poor. An original statue of Saint Anthony still stands at the mission today.

◀ *Saint Anthony of Padua.*

The Mission System

The mission system under the Franciscans was different. Instead of just sending religious missionaries, the Spanish government sent both soldiers and friars (called *frays* in Spanish). The soldiers were there to enforce rules and keep the peace, while the friars taught the Indians Christianity and turned them into good Spanish citizens. The soldiers lived in military fortresses, called presidios, and the friars lived in quarters within the mission complex. Each mission also included a church that was the center of mission life. The missionaries were to attract American Indians to the missions and teach them Spanish farming and work methods so that they could help build the mission structures and farm the land. The friars never thought that the land belonged to them. They planned to return it to the Indians once the Indians had become Spanish citizens.

Ideas Behind the Mission System

There were several ideas behind the mission system. Religion was one cause. During the time Spain started founding the missions, it was largely a Catholic country. This means that the Spanish people followed the teachings of Catholicism, which is a type of Christianity. Catholics believed that only people who practiced the Catholic faith would go to heaven. Missionaries wanted to spread Christianity to people in other countries. The Indians who lived at the missions and learned about Christianity were called neophytes.

At the time the mission system was established, many Europeans believed that the American Indians were not a very advanced people. The Indians had their own ways of living on the land, their own

The friars worked on the missions in order to spread the word of Christianity. ▶

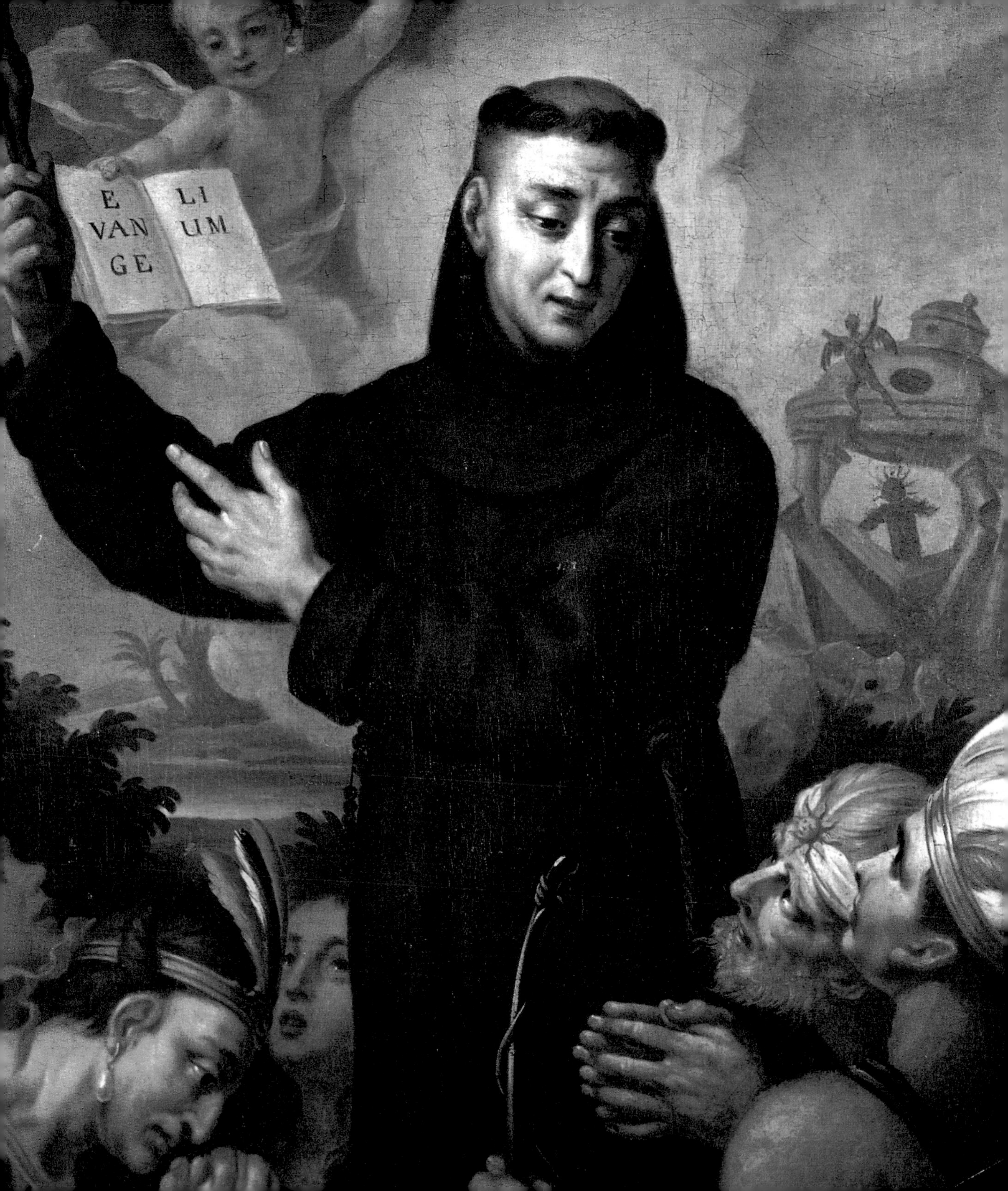
E VAN GE
LI UM

languages, and their own moral and spiritual beliefs. We know today that their civilization was different from the European way of life, but it was just as cultured and valuable.

Even though the missionaries who came to the New World to work at the missions had good intentions, they did not acknowledge that the Salinan Indians already had their own cultural and religious beliefs. Sadly, much of the Salinan's culture was lost because of the missions. The missions were not always places of peaceful interaction between friars and Indians. Sometimes, Indians who did not want to live at the missions were forced to stay by the soldiers. Some neophytes ran away from the mission. If the soldiers caught the escaped Indians, they brought them back and punished them.

The Spanish government also had political reasons for beginning the mission system. Spain knew that other countries were interested in the land called Alta (or "upper") California. If Spain built missions there, they would have a way to defend the land against these other empires. Once they gathered people to join the missions, the Spanish would have extra help to build and farm the mission lands, which would save them money and effort.

The Spanish government planned to secularize the missions. This means that they would make the missions nonreligious and that the settlements would be run by the government. By training American Indians in Spanish ways and involving them in mission life, Spain would make them into Spanish citizens. That way, when they secularized the missions and turned the land over to the neophytes, Spain would automatically have control over the land.

◀ *The Spanish did not respect the Salinan Indians' way of life.*

The Salinan Indians

When the Spanish arrived in the area where Mission San Antonio de Padua was eventually built, there were about 20 Salinan villages living there. Today, there is little known about the Salinan Indians. Even the original name of their tribe is not known. The name Salinan was given to them by the Spanish. The name comes from the Salinas River, which flows through the area where they lived.

▲

The Salinan used rocks like this one to grind acorns.

Salinan Indians lived off the land around them. They lived in thatched houses with their entire families. They ate fish, reptiles, birds, and other small animals. The men in the tribe hunted these animals with bows and arrows made from wood, stone, and animal hides. In California, there are many different kinds of plants that can be eaten. The Indians gathered acorns, grass, berries, nuts, grapes, and even prickly pears. The women in the tribe made a mush out of the acorns by grinding them and then cooking them. The Salinan ate this oatmeal-like food with their hands. Sometimes they baked acorn breads with the ground acorn flour. Since raw acorns are poisonous, though, they had to be careful to clean the acorns before eating them.

The Salinan women gathered grasses in clay bowls. ▶

They did this by washing the acorn flour 10 times with water.

The Salinan Indians also made whatever clothes they wore out of animal hides. Since it was so hot during the summers, men and children wore nothing. Women wore an apron with a front and back

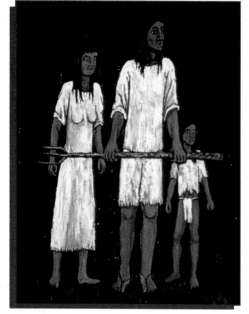

and a fringe cut into the bottom. Often, these skirts were made out of tree bark that was strung onto a cord. The women sometimes wore caps that looked like baskets. These caps helped them carry heavy loads on their heads. During the winter, the Salinan Indians wore robes or blankets to keep warm. These robes were made out of the skins of deer, wildcat, and sea otter. The Salinan usually did not wear shoes and often decorated themselves with ear ornaments or red and yellow body paint.

▲

This painting was done by an Indian at Mission San Antonio.

Before the missionaries came to California, the Salinan practiced their own religion. They had advisors who they believed could communicate with the gods. These advisors were called shamans. In the Salinan tribe only men could be shamans. Each tribe might have many different shamans. One might be a weather shaman, who they believed could control the weather. Another might be in charge of curing the sick.

Although the Salinan were usually peaceful, they fought occasionally

▲

Indians living at the mission dressed in the Spanish style.

with other tribes. Generally the Ohlone Indians who lived to the north were their enemies. They traded goods such as animal hides or hard-to-find stones with the Chumash people in the south.

When the Spanish arrived in California, the lifestyle of the Salinan changed forever. Not only are there very few members of this tribe left, but much of their culture was lost as a result of the mission system.

The Journey to San Antonio

Spain's vision was to establish a mission trail along the coast of California, beginning in San Diego and continuing up to what is now northern California. San Antonio de Padua was the third of these missions.

To found each mission the Spanish government sent two Franciscan friars and several soldiers and military leaders. Each mission was given $1,000 in Spanish money to pay for supplies. The first missions were established in Baja California. (Baja California means "lower" California, but it actually refers to a peninsula that is now part of Mexico.) When the Jesuits were told to leave the missions, an army captain named Gaspár de Portolá was made the governor of Baja California and Alta California. The Spanish government believed that the Jesuit missions were very rich, but Portolá found that they were run down.

Fray Serra was the most important figure in the founding of the missions. ▶

Portolá was born in Balaguer, Spain, in 1723. He joined the military when he was very young. In 1769 he led the first expedition from New Spain to Alta California to claim the land for Spain. Accompanying Portolá on this expedition was a Franciscan friar named Junípero Serra. Serra would become the most important figure in the founding of the Alta California missions.

Gáspar de Portolá led the expedition to Alta California. ▶

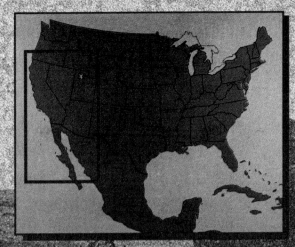

Alta
California

New Spain

Baja
California

Pacific
Ocean

Baja Penninsula

Junípero Serra was born on the island of Majorca, Spain, on November 24, 1713. His parents named him Miguel Joseph Serra. Although his parents were farmers, Serra showed great interest in learning about Catholicism. He learned to read and write at a nearby Franciscan friary. When he was 15, his parents sent him to a Franciscan school in the capital of Majorca. At 16, Serra took his vows to join the Franciscans.

When a young man becomes a Franciscan, he chooses a new name for himself. Serra chose the name Junípero in honor of a close friend and follower of Saint Francis (the founder of the Francsican order). Serra became a priest in 1737 and worked teaching philosophy in Spain. He knew that he wanted to teach other people about the Catholic religion. Even though he was successful in Spain, Serra decided that he wanted to be a missionary in the New World.

Once he arrived in New Spain, Serra insisted on walking all the way to the capital, Mexico City. Serra was a small, frail man. During the trip, Serra's leg became infected. He had problems as a result of this injury for the rest of his life.

Serra worked in New Spain teaching and giving sermons until 1769, when he was chosen to be president of the California missions. He was already 55 years old but was eager to begin converting the Indians of Alta California. He began an expedition to San Diego in the spring. The journey was a very hard one. By the time Serra and his crew arrived, half of the people in their group had died.

Fray Serra established the first mission, Mission San Diego de Alcalá, on July 16, 1769. In all, Serra founded nine missions in Alta

◀ *Fray Serra.*

California during his lifetime. He died on August 28, 1784, at his headquarters in Mission San Carlos Borromeo del Río Carmelo.

Other friars and missionaries served along with Fray Serra to found Mission San Antonio de Padua, including Fray Miguel Pieras. Pieras began his work at the mission in 1771, when he was only 30 years old. He barely ever left the grounds until he retired to Mexico in 1793.

Fray Bonaventure Sitjar also played an important role in the development of the mission. He was born in 1739 in Majorca, Spain. When Fray Pieras left the mission, Fray Sitjar took charge. He stayed at the mission for the rest of his life and is credited with many accomplishments, including putting together a grammar and vocabulary book of the American Indian language spoken in the area.

A drawing of Mission San Antonio. ▶

Founding Mission
San Antonio de Padua

On July 14, 1771, Mission San Antonio de Padua was founded. Fray Serra, Fray Sitjar, Fray Pieras, several soldiers, and two converted Indian families from Baja California entered an area called the Valley of the Oaks. This valley is located east of the coastline, in the foothills

A mission bell like this one hung at Mission San Antonio de Padua.

of the Santa Lucias Mountain range. The area had fertile soil and was close to a river and many friendly Indians. Fray Serra found a spot along the river and officially began Mission San Antonio by hanging a bell in an oak tree. He rang the bell in order to attract the local Indians. Serra cried out "Hear, oh Gentiles, come oh come, to Holy Church!" The other people on the expedition told Serra that no one was around for miles and that no one would come. Serra said that he wanted to express his feelings about Christianity. Ringing the bell had a special meaning to him. It was a symbol of his desire to teach everyone and let the whole world hear about the Christian religion.

Then, the people on the expedition built a temporary altar and raised a cross. Serra held the first service in the Valley of the Oaks and named the mission in honor of Saint Anthony of Padua. One story of the mission's founding says that when Serra turned from the altar to begin preaching, he saw a young American Indian boy who had heard the ringing of the bell. Fray Serra was overjoyed. It was the first

This is what the original gateway of San Antonio de Padua looked like.

25

time that an Indian had been present at the founding of a mission. As soon as Mass was over, the friars gave the boy small gifts, which they hoped would attract other Indians.

The friars would often give Indians gifts of beads, trinkets, food, and clothing. Christianity was probably not the reason most Indians were attracted to the missions. They were curious about these new people and fascinated by the gifts that they had brought. The friars invited the Indians to watch as they began building.

After the first service at Mission San Antonio, the building began immediately. The Salinan Indians were friendly and offered to help build the first mission structures. These shelters were very simple. Usually young trees were used as posts and then poles were put on top as a roof. Branches or tule, a kind of reed, were laid on top. The Salinan were drawn to the European tools, such as hammers and axes, that the missionaries used. The Indians also provided advice for their visitors. They knew where to find the best tule and showed the Spanish. An Indian who helped the friars was often rewarded with gifts and trinkets.

It was easier for the missionaries of San Antonio de Padua to recruit neophytes than it was for the friars at other missions. The American Indians in the areas surrounding Mission San Antonio de Padua and the Catholics had similar ideas about gods and deities. Even though there is no record of any Europeans visiting this land before, the Salinan Indians told the Spanish settlers that their legends were about bearded men dressed like Spaniards who had visited their land in earlier times. The Salinan even showed the missionaries a cave full of drawings and carvings of Indian gods along with what look like Christian crosses.

This cave was decorated by the Chumash Indians, a tribe who lived near the Salinan. ▶

This cave is still preserved today. This familiarity may explain why the Salinan Indians accepted the Catholic conversions peacefully, while other tribes were not as willing to become a part of the Christian life.

The missionaries and neophytes started building Mission San Antonio in 1771, almost immediately after its founding. The original structures were built along the river, but a year and a half later that part of the river ran dry. There was not enough water to take care of everyone at the mission. In 1773, the mission was moved to a new location. At this new spot, about a mile up the river, there was water all year. This location was in the Valley of Oaks at a point on the river called San Miguel Creek.

Many missions had to be moved because the land would not produce good crops. Each mission had to produce all its own food, so the location was very important. After the move to San Miguel, there were still more problems for the inhabitants of Mission San Antonio de Padua. In the spring of 1780, the wheat crop was almost destroyed by a cold frost. The mission Indians flooded the fields to thaw the wheat. Then, everyone prayed for nine days that the crop would be saved. That year, the crop was better than ever before. This event gave many neophytes faith in the Christian religion.

Immediately after the move, everyone got to work putting up a small church and a few buildings. These buildings were made out of adobe bricks. Adobe was a mixture of mud, clay, straw, and sometimes manure. The adobe was packed into brick molds and then dried in the sun. The bricks were then covered in plaster to make them waterproof. After the plaster, the bricks were held together with mud. The buildings were given a coat of whitewash made of lime, goat's milk, and salt. The

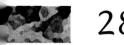

▲

*Adobe bricks
drying in
the sun.*

▲

Neophytes making adobe bricks.

neophytes also made tiles out of clay that they shaped with molds. The California Indians working at the mission could produce up to 500 tiles a day. There were also a few new houses made of wood that were constructed for the American Indians and soldiers. The mission was shaped like a rectangle that was centered around a courtyard. This shape was called a quadrangle. It was used in the missions in order to protect against the attacks of Indian tribes and also to create a close

▲

A view of the mission quadrangle from overhead.

community within the mission walls. A small garden was located to the side of the courtyard. The mission also included a wine cellar with huge wine vats, an olive press used to make olive oil, and several workshops where the neophytes could practice their newly learned trades.

Because Mission San Antonio de Padua was built along the San Antonio River, an irrigation system was built to supply water for the mission. The neophytes built a temporary dam out of stones, poles, and brushwood. Water was used to water crops, to power the gristmill, and for bathing, washing, and cooking. Later, a more permanent dam was built out of rocks.

Building continued for almost the entire mission period. In fact, the mission church structure wasn't even started until 1810 and wasn't completed and blessed until 1813. This long-awaited structure is still standing today. San Antonio de Padua is now one of the largest and most accurately restored missions.

The aqueduct reached from the river to the gristmill.

To run the gristmill, water poured out of the pipe, forcing the wheel to turn. This rotated the stone that ground the flour.

31

Life at the Mission

By 1773, there was already a population of almost 200 people involved with Mission San Antonio de Padua. This was an unusually high number for a mission in its beginning years. Eventually more Salinan Indians moved to the mission. Others lived at their own villages, coming to the mission on a daily basis for work, food, and education. The Salinan Indians were taught Catholicism, the Spanish language, and music. They were also trained in European ways of working. Plowing fields, for instance, was an entirely new skill that the mission Indians learned.

In 1775, an attack on the mission threatened the peace of the new community. During a baptism, a group of Indians from outside the mission began shooting arrows at the mission inhabitants. The man being baptized was wounded, but when he recovered from his injuries, some of the neophytes believed it was a sign. They thought that the mission's patron saint, Saint Anthony, had saved the baptized man. Even though the attack could have had a horrible effect on the Indians' feelings about the mission, life at Mission San Antonio continued undisturbed.

The daily schedule at the mission was very strict and had to be obeyed by everyone who was not ill. This was a very different way of life for the mission Indians. Before moving to the mission, the Salinan were free to do what they wanted. At the mission, everyone had to work to feed, clothe, and provide for every other person. This was part of the friars' plan to make the mission a successful community. It was difficult for many Salinan to adapt. Some Indians did not want to give up their personal freedom to join the mission. Others did not realize how demanding mission life would be until it was too late and they were forced to stay.

◀ *Mission San Antonio de Padua had two bells, each used for a different purpose.*

A typical day at Mission San Antonio de Padua was organized around the ringing of the mission bells. There were two bells at every mission. One bell rang to tell those living at the mission that it was time to say prayers. Another bell rang to signal the times for work, rest, or meals. At sunrise a bell rang to awaken the mission inhabitants. Everyone at the mission came together for breakfast, usually consisting of *atole*, or corn porridge. After breakfast, everyone assembled in church for prayers. Then boys went to their classes and everyone else went to work on their specific duties and jobs.

The men went to work in the workshops or in the fields. They grew vegetables like corn, beans, and peas. The men also grew fruit trees and took care of the livestock. The women prepared meals. Cooking was mainly done over an open fire. Three large stones were set around the fire and a pot was placed on top. In the neophytes' village there was also an oven for baking bread. Some women worked at weaving and made fine blankets and cloth out of cotton, wool, and flax. Others made candles or wove baskets for use at the mission. Everything that was used at the mission had to be made by the people who lived there, so there were jobs for everyone.

▲
The women used a loom to weave blankets and clothes.

After chores, it was time for lunch. Lunch was usually a stew of wheat, corn, or beans called *pozole*. In addition to the food that the Salinan ate with the community, every family would have a pottage, a mixture of wild seeds, that they made in their own homes. Just as they had done before living at the mission, the Indians stored these seeds in large baskets or in granaries that they kept outside. Afterwards, everyone went back to work until dinner and another church service. Although it conflicted with the Catholic way

The Indians sang their own songs in addition to the religious ones they were taught. ▶

of life, the missionaries sometimes allowed the Indians to sing their own songs and also dance as they had before so that they would be content living at the mission.

Getting all the Indians' clothing took the missionaries a long time, but it was an important part of the missionaries' attempts to "civilize" the Salinan. The Indians didn't always like the idea of wearing clothes, but the missionaries insisted on this change. Men were given a blanket, a long shirt called a tunic, and a cloth to wrap around the waist called a breechcloth. Later, most of the men would also wear pants. Women were given a blanket, a tunic, and a skirt.

Eventually, many missionaries decided to let the Indians they trusted make short visits to their homes. Without these visits, many neophytes

The Indians were baptized when they were accepted into the Christian faith.

would become unhappy. These vacations were considered to be "necessary evils" by the friars. They didn't want to let the neophytes go, but they also wanted to keep them happy.

When an Indian was baptized, he was told that he would have to follow the rules of the mission. One way that the friars made sure that the Indians would not go back to their old ways was to divide families into married couples, girls, and boys. Married couples and their young children lived in small villages, called *rancherías*, a short distance from the main mission buildings. Older children were taken from their parents so that they would not learn the traditional Salinan ways.

At eight years old, girls were taken to different quarters called *monjerios*. Widows and young unmarried women also lived there. The girls were locked into their dormitories at night. When they slept, an older, trusted person watched them. This person was a Christian woman called a *maestra*. The *maestra* would also assign the girls tasks to do during the day. The girls were not allowed to leave their dormitories until they had completed their work. Afterwards, they would be allowed to visit the village.

At that time in Spain, it was common to keep young women locked in their rooms at night. Spanish parents guarded their daughters and slept in adjoining rooms. The friars kept the girls closely watched to make sure that they would be raised according to Christian and European ideals. When they were old enough to be married, the women moved into the village with their husbands. Boys also lived in separate quarters, but they were not locked up at night. The friars looked after the boys. From these boys, the friars would choose their servants, bell ringers, pages, choirboys, and musicians. Other boys would become blacksmiths, tanners, farmers, carpenters, masons, or herdsmen, called *vaqueros*.

One big problem that the missionaries did not predict was the effect of European diseases on the Indians. When Europeans came to the New World, they brought with them diseases the Indians had never been exposed to, such as measles, mumps, and smallpox. Many Indians became ill and died. The friars were unable to cure all of the sick, and populations at the missions dropped as a result.

The Decline of Mission San Antonio de Padua

The 1800s began a period of hardship at Mission San Antonio de Padua. More neophytes were dying at the mission than were being born. Others were afraid of the soldiers, who sometimes acted cruelly. Many Indians were angry because their freedom had been taken from them. The rules were very strict, and disobedient neophytes were whipped, put into the stocks, or made to wear chains. The stocks were a device that punished a person by holding their hands and feet in one place.

At some missions, the Indians were held captive. They had to work to support the mission system and had limited choices in their daily lives. If a neophyte broke the rules or ran away and was brought back again, he would first be reminded that he had chosen to live in the mission and promised to follow the rules. If he broke the rules again, he was punished by flogging or whipping. The third time a neophyte broke the rules, he would be forced to wear heavy chains while he worked. Women were usually punished with one, two, or three days in the stocks. All of these punishments were considered appropriate by the missionaries. They believed that the Indians were like children and didn't have the same rights as everyone else.

Another problem with the mission system was that the soldiers did not always behave according to the mission's standards. The soldiers were supposed to uphold the rules, but instead they sometimes broke them. There are reports of soldiers stealing from, abusing, wrongly punishing, and sometimes attacking Indians. One reason for these problems was that the soldiers were not at the mission for the same

At many missions, Indians were punished for disobedience by whipping or flogging. ▶

reasons as the friars, and they did not care for the Indians. In the end, however, both soldiers and some friars were responsible for the neophytes' mistreatment.

In 1810, the people of New Spain began a revolution against the Spanish government to gain their independence. While the Spanish government was busy trying to stop rebels in Mexico, it neglected to send supplies to the missions. As a result, some soldiers did not receive their pay from the government and stole from the neophytes. The soldiers began to cause more and more trouble at Mission San Antonio de Padua.

In 1821, the people of New Spain won the war and formed the new nation of Mexico. Alta and Baja California became parts of Mexico. In 1833, the Mexican government decided to secularize the missions, but not the way the Spanish had initially intended. A commissioner was assigned to each mission and was put in charge of managing the American Indians and their education. The friars were put on a salary and were now held responsible only for the religious training of the Indians. Each male Indian over 20 years old was supposed to be given 33 acres of land. Half of the mission's tools, livestock, and seeds were also supposed to be given to the men. An Indian who accepted this land was forced by the government to work the land. In many cases, the Indians decided that they didn't like this deal. They decided to flee the mission and live on their own. Mexican settlers moved into the area and began ranches. Some Indians worked on these ranches and were treated very badly by the Mexicans.

▲

By 1884, the mission had fallen into ruin.

In 1883, Mission San Antonio de Padua was abandoned. Sadly, the original tiles were stolen from the roof, and most of the walls crumbled. Mission San Antonio de Padua declined more than many

41

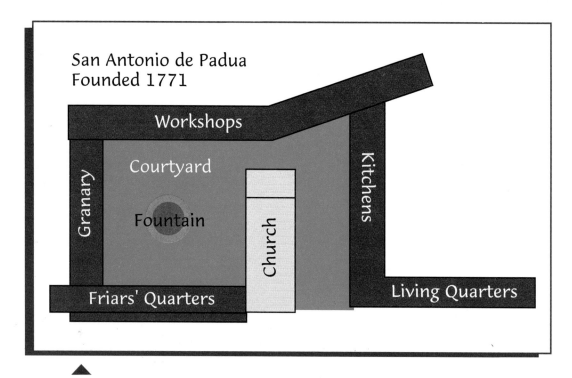

San Antonio de Padua
Founded 1771

Workshops

Courtyard

Granary

Fountain

Kitchens

Church

Friars' Quarters

Living Quarters

Architectural layout of the mission.

of the other Californian missions because it had fewer visitors in its remote location. From 1903 to 1908 an attempt to restore the mission was started, but only the church was restored. During the period from 1928 to 1984, the mission was turned back over to the Roman Catholic Church. Through the 1950s, the Franciscans returned and continued with restoration, and by July 14, 1971, the San Antonio de Padua Mission was able to celebrate its 200th Anniversary Bicentennial in a partially renovated form.

Several priests aided in the 1903 restoration. ▶

Mission San Antonio de Padua Today

The Legacy of Mission San Antonio de Padua

Mission San Antonio de Padua is one of the few California missions that is still functioning today. It is an active Catholic parish that is home to a priest and three Franciscan brothers. The mission holds daily masses for the community, and visitors are welcomed. The mission also houses an extensive museum where a visitor can walk into the original wine vat, which is the size of a whole room. Visitors can see parts of the living quarters set up as they were when the mission was first established by the friars.

People who visit the mission today are also able to see and touch much of the original plant life from the mission's early days. In the center of the mission building there is a beautiful garden. A grape vine, grown from the seeds of an original grape vine, still grows in the garden. At the entrance to the mission is an olive tree from the 1830s, which still produces olives.

This olive tree has stood at the mission since the 1830s. ▶

◀ *Today, Fray John Gini leads the congregation at Mission San Antonio de Padua.*

The land around the mission is currently considered Fort Hunter-Liggett. The mission stands alone in the valley. There are no houses, restaurants, or hotels to be seen by the 25,000 visitors a year who come to see the mission. The visitors will often see one of the Franciscan brothers praying in the church, reading outside on the patio or walking around the grounds. Except for the occasional car that drives up to the mission, you almost feel like you have been transported to the time when Mission San Antonio de Padua was at its peak.

Unlike many of the other missions in California today, there are many artifacts from the original structures at Mission San Antonio de Padua. The mission's chapel houses many of the important original pieces of history. The original baptistery and tabernacle are located in the chapel, and on the altar sit many of the original statues, including those of Mary and Joseph, two important figures in Christianity. When the chapel was renovated, artwork, probably from the Santa Bárbara mission, was added to the

This statue of Joseph was preserved for many years.

This statue of Mary still stands in the mission's church.

◀ *Mission San Antonio de Padua today.*

47

▲

The mission pews today.

walls. Pews were also added. When the chapel existed in its early days, the American Indians sat on the floor during Mass and prayers. Written accounts and several photos taken in 1870 show us what the original mission church and most of the mission looked like before falling to ruins.

One interesting feature of the church at Mission San Antonio de Padua is the acoustics. The way a room is shaped and built determines how clearly sounds and music can be heard. From front to back, the church spans 245 feet, and there is a 45-foot distance from the floor to the ceiling and from wall to wall. These measurements make it possible for someone to stand at the front of the church by the altar and be heard loud and clear by someone

The original mission bell, which was made in Lima, Peru in 1799, still hangs over the mission. Like the Liberty Bell in Philadelphia, the mission's bell is cracked but it has remained well preserved.

The original mission bell.

standing all the way at the back of the chapel, even if he or she speaks very softly. This is even more incredible because this is a feature of the original church. The structure of the chapel has remained the same from before the renovation. It is truly amazing that the friars, soldiers, and American Indians who built the church, having no access to the modern tools and measuring devices we have today, were able to construct such a masterpiece of a building.

Like the mission buildings, Mission San Antonio de Padua's story has survived as a reminder of the past. Just as it was the birthplace of many California "firsts," it is today a lasting monument representing two different cultures and the contacts and conflicts that made the population of California what it is today.

◀ *The mission church is still used today.*

Make Your Own Mission
San Antonio de Padua

To make your own model of the San Antonio de Padua mission, you will need:

Styrofoam
red, green, black, and terracotta paint
toothpicks
ruler
dry lasagna
flowers

foamcore board
bell
trees
glue

Directions

Step 1: Cut two church walls (front and back) out of foamcore board. Paint all sides with terracotta paint.

6.75"   4.75"

7.75"

Step 2: Cut two church walls (sides) out of foamcore board. Paint all sides with terracotta paint.

4.75"

12.5"

Adult supervision is suggested.

Step 3: Cut two roof panels out of foamcore board. Paint all sides with red paint.

4.75"

12.5"

Step 4: Cut one courtyard wall (side) out of styrofoam. Paint all sides with terracotta paint. Paint doors with black paint.

2.5"

11"

Step 5: Cut two courtyard walls (front and back) out of styrofoam. Paint all sides with terracotta paint. Paint doors with black paint.

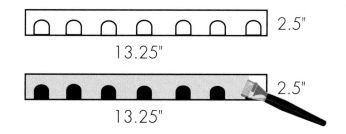

2.5"

13.25"

2.5"

13.25"

Step 6: Cut one church wall (front facade) out of foamcore. Paint all sides with terracotta paint. Paint doors with black paint. Cut a hole out to hang bell.

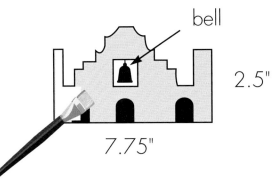

bell

2.5"

7.75"

Step 7: For the base material, cut a piece of cardboard. Paint courtyard area with green paint; paint sidewalk with terracotta paint.

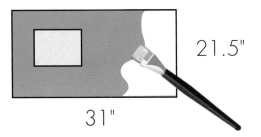

21.5"

31"

Step 8: Glue together (corner to corner) the four walls, that were cut in steps 1 and 2. Wait for glue to dry.

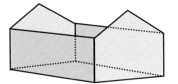

Step 9: Glue the two roof panels that were cut in step 3 to the top of the church. Wait for glue to dry.

Step 10: Glue the front and back courtyard walls, cut in step 4, to the sides of the church. Wait for glue to dry.

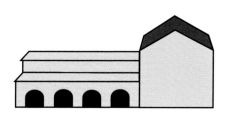

Step 11: Glue the church wall, cut in step 5, to the front of the church structure. Wait for glue to dry.

Step 12: Glue the church wall, cut in step 6, to the front of the church structure. Wait for glue to dry.

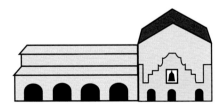

Step 13: Paint lasagna red and glue to the roof panels. Wait for glue to dry.

Step 14: Glue entire structure to base material that was cut in step 7. Wait for glue to dry.

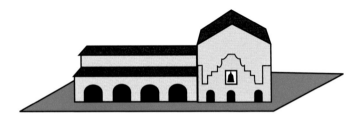

Step 15: Use a toothpick to attach bell. Glue two toothpicks together to make a cross. Wait for glue to dry. Glue cross to the top front of the church. Wait for glue to dry. Decorate the mission with flowers and trees as you want it to look.

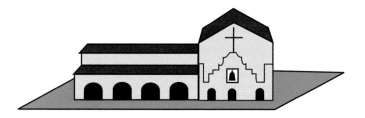

*Use the above mission as a reference for building your mission.

Important Dates in Mission History

1492	Christopher Columbus reaches the West Indies
1542	Cabrillo's expedition to California
1602	Sebastián Vizcaíno sails to California
1713	Fray Junípero Serra is born
1769	Founding of San Diego de Alcalá
1770	Founding of San Carlos Borromeo del Río Carmelo
1771	**Founding of San Antonio de Padua** and San Gabriel Arcángel
1772	Founding of San Luis Obispo de Tolosa
1775–76	Founding of San Juan Capistrano
1776	Founding of San Francisco de Asís
1776	Declaration of Independence is signed
1777	Founding of Santa Clara de Asís
1782	Founding of San Buenaventura
1784	Fray Serra dies
1786	Founding of Santa Bárbara Virgen y Mártir
1787	Founding of La Purísima Concepción de Maria Santísima
1791	Founding of Santa Cruz and Nuestra Señora de la Soledad
1797	Founding of San José, San Juan Bautista, San Miguel Arcángel, and San Fernando Rey de España
1798	Founding of San Luis Rey de Francia
1804	Founding of Santa Inés Virgen y Mártir
1817	Founding of San Rafael Arcángel
1823	Founding of San Francisco de Solano
1849	Gold found in northern California
1850	California becomes the 31st state

Glossary

adobe (uh-DOH-bee) Sun-dried bricks made of straw, mud, and sometimes manure.

artifact (AR-tih-fact) An object made by humans, often used by scientists and historians to learn more about the people and time when they were made.

baptistery (bap-TIS-ter-ee) Part of a church (or a separate building) used for baptisms.

Catholicism (kuh-THAH-lih-sih-zum) The faith or practice of Catholic Christianity, which includes following the spiritual leadership of priests headed by a pope.

Christianity (kris-chee-AN-ih-tee) A religion based on the teachings of Jesus Christ and the Bible, practiced by Eastern, Roman Catholic, and Protestant groups.

colonization (kah-luh-nih-ZAY-shun) Setting up a community of settlers as a means of taking over land.

convert (kun-VIRT) To change from belief in one religion to belief in another religion.

culture (KUL-cher) The skills, customs, arts, and beliefs of a civilization.

Franciscan (fran-SIS-kin) A communal Roman Catholic order of friars, or "brothers" who follow the teachings and example of Saint Francis of Assisi, who did much work as a missionary.

friar (FRY-ur) A brother in a communal religious order. Friars can also be priests.

irrigation (ih-rih-GAY-shun) A way of supplying water through artificial ditches.

neophyte (NEE-oh-fyt) The name for an American Indian right after converting to the Christian faith.

quarters (KWOR-turz) Rooms where someone lives.

restoration (reh-stuh-RAY-shun) Working to return something, such as a building, to its original state.

secularization (seh-kyoo-luh-rih-ZAY-shun) The process by which the missions were made to be nonreligious.

tabernacle (TA-ber-na-kul) A house of worship.

villages (VIH-luh-jez) Original communities where American Indians lived before the arrival of the Spanish. Non-Christian and non-mission Indians continued to live in these villages.

Pronunciation Guide

atole (ah-TOL-ay)

El Camino Real (EL kah-MEE-noh ray-AL)

fray (FRAY)

maestras (my-es-TRAHZ)

monjerío (mohn-HAYR-ee-oh)

pozole (poh-ZOHL-ay)

rancherías (RAHN-cher-EE-as)

vaqueros (bah-KEHR-ohs)

Resources

For more information on Mission San Antonio de Padua and the California missions, check out these books and Web sites.

Books:

Casey, Beatrice. *Padres & People of Old Mission San Antonio*. King City, CA: Casey Newspapers, 1976. (Available through mission.)

Sprietsma, Leo. *Manuscript for a New History of Mission San Antonio de Padua*. Mission San Antonio. (Available through mission.)

Lowman, Hubert. The Old Spanish Missions of California.

Web Sites:

www.missionsanantoniopadua.com (Official Mission Web Site)

For further information about Mission San Antonio de Padua, or for pamphlets, brochures and photos distributed at the mission, contact the San Antonio de Padua Mission directly at:

      P.O. Box 803
      Jolon, California 93928
      Phone: 408-385-4478

Index

Author Acknowledgments

As always, thanks to my supportive family. Very special thanks to Dennis Linders, the incredibly knowledgeable manager of the gift shop at Mission San Antonio, for taking so much time to show me around the mission and for sharing so much of his vast knowledge about the mission with me.